Norman Rockwell's AMERICAN CHILDREN

Written by Marian Hoffman

CRESCENT BOOKS
New York

Norman Rockwell's American Children

Illustrations reprinted under license from
the Estate of Norman Rockwell.

Copyright © 1990 Estate of Norman Rockwell

Photographic material courtesy of
The Norman Rockwell Museum at
Stockbridge, Stockbridge, MA

Created and manufactured by arrangement with
Ottenheimer Publishers, Inc.

Copyright © 1990 Ottenheimer Publishers, Inc.
This 1990 edition is published by Ottenheimer
Publishers, Inc. for Crescent Books,
distributed by Crown Publishers, Inc.,
225 Park Avenue South, New York, New York 10003

Printed and bound in Hong Kong.

ISBN: 0-517-03172-8
h g f e d c b a

Contents

Children Dancing at Party (1918)

Introduction

Matthew sleeps at night in the same bed his father slept in as a boy—a wooden captain's bed that Matthew's grandfather built. The bed is only one of many threads that connect Matthew's childhood to his parents' and even his grandparents' childhoods. For the qualities of childhood are timeless, and even the day-to-day rituals remain remarkably the same for children several generations apart. Fashions and fads change, but the elements that fill up a child's day, and the thoughts that fill his mind, remain much the same.

At home, children have meal time, chore time, bath time, sparring with sibling time, play time, and snuggle time. Their day-to-day rituals include school, music lessons, visits with friends, homework, and church.

Children of all generations experience the same rites of growing up. Matthew's first loose tooth dangles at an angle for days, while his tongue wiggles it incessantly. The tooth finally comes out and is stashed under his pillow, waiting for booty from the tooth fairy. William watches his father shave and will someday, not really that far in the future, experience his first shave. Julia puts on Mom's lipstick and checks in the mirror to see if she looks more glamorous and grown up.

These are the images of childhood that Norman Rockwell depicts in his paintings—images that are timeless and universal. In his many portrayals of children, Norman Rockwell captures the everyday trivia as well as the underlying spirit of children's lives.

"Foller the Leader"

Foller the Leader (1919)

Chapter 1
Pastimes

Chilton Road

Matthew, William and Julia lived at 2310 Chilton Road, a gray-shingled house in the middle of the block. There were at least fourteen other children between the ages of six and twelve living on the 2300 block of Chilton. Five of them belonged to the Preston family—the Prestons had eight children in all—the rest were distributed evenly among the remaining houses.

After school, on weekends, and after dinner on sultry summer evenings, the "Chilton Road Gang" gathered on the street. Sometimes they roller skated or bicycled, but frequently they congregated at the Prestons, whose house was nestled down in the woods. Surrounding the house was a split-rail fence, which did double duty as the neighborhood balance beam. The children took turns trying to walk the length of the fence without tumbling over. Matthew held Julia's hand until she became steady enough to navigate the rail alone. Butch Preston, the oldest of the bunch, could make it from one end to the other at breakneck speed, and was working on perfecting tricks involving hops and jumps.

When the children tired of fence walking, they ran into the woods to explore. A big tree that had fallen across the stream was used as a bridge. William liked to pretend he was lost and had to find his way out of the jungle. Several times a summer, Matthew and Julia became covered with poison ivy from the Preston's woods. Their mother sat them in the kitchen on an old army blanket and covered them from head to toe with calamine lotion. William, who played in the woods all the time, never got poison ivy, which didn't seem quite fair to his siblings.

Philip Winter's parents allowed the Chilton Street Gang to use their front yard as the neighborhood ball field. It wasn't a very large yard, but it was level. Level yards were hard to come by on Chilton Street, because the houses on one side of the street were perched on a hill, and the ones on the other side were nestled in the woods. In the fall, the children played touch football; in the spring, they played baseball. Soon there wasn't a blade of grass remaining on the Winter's front yard.

Matthew, William, and Julia's house had the distinction of having the best steps for step-ball games. Their house was high on a hill, with many front steps that were at just the right angle to get the best bounce out of a ball. Every spring, when their mother was gardening, she would find dozens of rubber balls nestled in the undergrowth. Matthew kept the extra balls in a bag hanging by the basement door, and the other kids knew that they could always dig into the bag for a replacement if they lost their last ball.

Off to School (1920)

The New Kid

William was eight when Marty moved into the neighborhood. Marty was eight too, and an only child. He lived with his mother, father, and grandmother in the green, split-level house at the end of the block.

Maybe it was because Marty's house was tucked away at the end of the street; maybe it was because the green house was a little strange; or maybe it was because Marty was the only child in a house of three adults. Whatever the reason, the neighborhood kids didn't pay much attention to Marty and he had a hard time being accepted by the gang.

Marty hung on the edges of the group, circling around their games on his skates or bike. One day, when William and Suzy Winter were walking home from school, Marty did a headstand right in front of them, so they couldn't help but notice. Suzy was impressed, but William tried not to pay too much attention.

Marty's house had one thing that no one else's did—it had a long, paved driveway leading to double garage doors. One day Philip saw Marty's father hanging a *real* basketball net on the garage doors. Sometimes the kids had dunked balls into garbage cans in the alley, but there had never been a suitable place for a real basketball net before.

On Wednesday, after school, the Chilton Street Gang headed for Marty's house. Suzy had baked some brownies with her Mom, which she carried over in a red tin with a picture of a roaring hearth on it. They introduced themselves to Marty's parents and grandmother, and asked Marty if they could try out his new net. After that, basketball became one of the gang's regular activities, and Marty became a regular member of the group.

Cousin Reginald is Cut Out (1917)

Diss-Honor—A Peg Story (1918)

And Not to Be Outdone

William pretended that Marty's headstand made no impression on him, but that wasn't really the truth. He had been attempting a headstand himself for quite some time, with little success. Because of Marty's achievement, William decided to step up his training.

He had tried the standard technique of balancing on his head while swinging his feet up quickly, but inevitably ended up flipping over. This time he decided to use the wall as a prop. He placed his hands and head on the floor and tried to walk his feet up the wall. The one advantage to this technique was that, thanks to the wall, there was only one direction William could fall in, and he had padded that area with cushions. The disadvantage was that it was impossible to show off outside to the other kids, since there were no walls to prop up against.

William's challenge was to find the perfect place in which to practice his headstands. There was lots of open space outside, and the grass provided a natural cushion for falls, but he ran the risk of being spotted by the others and being laughed at. Inside was difficult because there were many obstacles, and each time he fell and thudded on the floor, his parents would yell at him. With William's head at floor level, his dog, Charlie, felt obliged to lick his face.

Somehow, despite the pitfalls, William mastered the headstand, although it turned out to be a skill that wasn't as useful as he had expected. Marty, in the meantime, had gone on to cartwheels and double flips, and continued to impress Suzy Winter a great deal.

The Space Ship

The gang decided to build a space ship in Matthew's back yard. They each went home and rummaged through their basements and garages to see what useful objects they could find. Butch brought a big wooden barrel, Matthew an orange crate, Philip a waste basket, Marty a broomstick, and William a funnel. Suzy and Julia found scraps of wood, in different shapes. Everyone came back with a hammer and all kinds of nails—some too long, some too short. Nobody's father except Butch's would let them have a saw, which was okay since no one could really saw that well anyway.

Everyone set to work except William. He was already dressed in his space helmet, and was carrying his space gun. "Is it finished yet?" he kept asking. Or, for a change of pace, he'd say, "*When* will it be finished?" He was not the least bit interested in making the space ship, but was impatient for it to be finished so he could play in it.

Nails were very popular among the workers. Matthew and Philip hammered dozens of nails into each piece of wood; they'd put twenty nails into an area that only really needed two or three. Few of the nails went in straight, and few of them had any structural importance. However, the boys thought all the shiny nailheads looked very impressive—they subscribed to the theory if one nail is good, then ten nails are better.

The orange crate became the base of the space ship. Next came the barrel, topped by an upside down waste basket. The funnel slid onto the broomstick to make the nose of the rocket. The girls' wood scraps became the fins. Butch sawed a hole into the barrel so they could crawl in. The space ship was almost finished.

Space Ship (1959-1960)   19

In fact, William and Philip considered it to be finished and started trying to crawl in. Matthew and Butch, however, were perfectionists and wanted to put on the finishing touches. Butch brought over cans of red and blue paint and a couple paintbrushes, and he and Matthew painted designs and insignias on the space ship.

The space ship stayed in the back yard for a long time. It became a sort of secret hideout for the boys. They would stash secret messages to each other inside, or use it as a meeting place to trade baseball cards and swap Hardy Boys books. Matthew's father grumbled about it being in the way, and being hard to mow around, but left it alone until the elements made it rusty and warped, and a general eyesore. By the time the space ship was hauled away, the boys had moved on to other interests and other projects. But they still felt a pang when the ship was dismantled, because it had been their first project—the very first thing they had conceived and implemented themselves.

The Climbing Tree

Matthew always thought there was something special about the oak tree. It was right in the middle of the back yard, and Matthew's bedroom windows looked directly on it. At first, Matthew was a little afraid of the tree. It was so big, Matthew wondered if it would fall in on his bed if the tree were hit by lightning. Sometimes he would hide in the walk-in closet during a bad thunderstorm, so the tree wouldn't topple on him while he was sleeping.

As he got older, however, the tree became his friend. It was an old tree, with branches spreading in all directions. Near the bottom of the trunk was a little hole, where Matthew kept special treasures that he didn't want William and Julia to get their hands on. Sometimes he read under the tree, with his back propped up against the trunk, and sometimes he played solitary make-believe games under the tree, pretending that the shiny bits of coal found under the tree were really buried treasure.

But the best thing about the tree was that it was perfect for climbing. The branches started low enough that even Julia could boost herself into the tree. The branches then continued at fairly even intervals, so Matthew could climb high enough to feel secluded. Of course, all the neighborhood children climbed in the tree too. It was by far the best climbing tree on the block. Matthew's dad hung a tire swing on one of the branches, and a wooden platform at the intersection of two other branches. Matthew had always intended to build a large treehouse in the oak, a fancy one like he had seen in a book once. But he never got around to it.

Marsha Preston got punished once for climbing the tree in her Sunday clothes, and once Ricky Winter took a fall from the third branch. However, tree-related mishaps were few and far between. When Matthew wanted to be alone, he would climb halfway up the tree and try to hide himself behind the leaves. His mother, watching from the kitchen window as she prepared dinner, could see him nestled up there, but Matthew never knew that he could be seen. It was his secret, special place.

One spring, Matthew's parents decided to sell the house and move to another one. To leave his tree, Matthew felt, was like moving away from a best friend. To his relief, his folks decided to stay on Chilton Road after all, and the tree remained a comfortable presence throughout Matthew's childhood.

Diss-Honor—A Peg Story (1918)

23

Playing Pirates

Fueled by their success with the space ship, the gang decided to construct a pirate ship and play pirates. Soon the girls found the game not to thier liking and wandered off in other pursuits.

As with the space ship, everyone raided their homes for suitable props. Marty brought a lantern with a handle, so it could be carried around by the sneaky pirates. Matthew brought an empty bottle to use as a spy glass. Philip took a white sheet from his mother's linen closet to use as a sail, which turned out not to be a good idea. When his mother discovered that Philip had ruined a good sheet, he was punished and not allowed to play with the gang for the rest of the week.

Butch's mother lent the boys some scarves, which they tied around their heads pirate-fashion. William had gotten a real pirate's outfit for Christmas, complete with eye patch and black hat. He wore the eye patch, but let Matthew, who was the captain, wear the hat.

Pirates Like These Need Triple Knees in Their Stockings (1924)

Everyone wanted to be the captain, of course, so they rolled the dice to see who got the highest number. Matthew won, but agreed to step down and give someone else a turn as captain after awhile.

Matthew found a long piece of lumber in the basement, which could be used as the gangplank. The boys each took turns being blindfolded and trying to walk the plank without falling off. Philip's dog, Ozzie, was upset by the blindfolds and the eye patches, and wouldn't stop barking. "It's just us, Ozzie," the boys kept saying, but the dog wasn't convinced. The barking got on their nerves, but there was something gratifying in knowing that their disguises were so convincing and menacing.

William suggested that they hunt for treasure, so they set off to see what they could find. They rounded up an impressive collection of rocks, bottle caps, and rubber bands. William found a penny. William was always finding pennies—on the street, in parking lots, in the grass. Matthew thought William found more coins than he did because William was shorter and, therefore, much closer to the ground.

Getting to School

Hamilton Elementary School was located on Hampton Avenue, at the foot of a very steep hill. All the neighborhood children walked to school, except on rainy days, when their dads would drop them off on the way to work. At 8:30 in the morning, the back doors of the houses on Chilton Road would open, and the children would set off to school—first to the end of Chilton, then a right on Fillow, and finally a left onto the Hampton Hill. At this hour of the morning, the sidewalk was bumper to bumper with youngsters. A crossing guard at the foot of the hill directed them across the street and into the school. Going home was more of a challenge, since the walk was uphill. When the sidewalk was icy, it was hard to get a footing. Once when it was icy, Wendy Simpson used the peg on the bottom of her cello as a crutch, to help hoist her up the hill.

The older kids went to Fallston Junior High, which was farther away than Hamilton Elementary, and in the other direction. They rode their bikes to school, or sometimes took the bus, which stopped a block away from Chilton Road. The bike riders rode to school, parked their bikes in the school bike rack, and locked them with a combination lock. Once Philip's older brother, Ned, locked his bike and forgot the combination. The school superintendent had to saw through the wire so Ned could get his bike out.

The boys carried their school books in a wire basket on the back of their bikes. Butch felt he needed a lot of equipment to keep his bike running. He always kept a pump on it in case of a flat tire on the way to school, but he had been lucky so far and had never needed it.

Butch thought bicycle bells were silly, and always had a collection of battery operated horns, chrome-plated things that never really worked the way they were supposed to. They either would stop working completely, or keep honking continuously and not turn off. Butch tried hitting the horns to silence them, but finally just took out the batteries. He went through a lot of horns, but never seemed to give up on them.

School, This Year, Means More Than Ever Before (1921)

The Television Set

After they were bathed and in their pajamas, the children were allowed to watch television before bedtime. Sometimes the entire family would gather around the set, watching a variety show. The children always sat right in front of the set, only a couple of feet away from it. "You're a better door than window," Dad would say. "You'll ruin your eyesight," Mom would add.

Television was the carrot dangled in front of the children. "Do your homework, and you can watch television." "Finish your chores, and you can watch television." "Don't hit your sister, or you won't be allowed to watch television." When Mom and Dad went out, the babysitter allowed the children to watch television past their bedtime. And sometimes, when they were in bed trying to fall asleep, they'd hear Mom and Dad watching television and strain to hear the words. The muffled sounds eventually lulled them to sleep.

The fights about television programs would start at the dinner table. One child wanted to watch westerns, the other wanted comedy shows. Mom and Dad would say, "if you can't agree, nobody will watch anything." Eventually a system was worked out, a rotating schedule that gave every member of the household a chance to watch a chosen show at least once a week.

When the *Wizard of Oz* came on television that year, practically all the residents of Chilton Road crowded around the Miller's set to see what Oz looked like in color. When Dorothy opened her door and there was Munchkinland, all in glorious color, everyone squealed with joy. Eventually, the other families on the block bought color sets, but none ever matched the grandeur of that mammoth console.

Enchanted Lands . . . Right in Your Home (c. 1950)

The Clock Fairy (1916)

Piano Practice

Suzy Winter was the first on the block to take piano lessons. Once a week, she went to Mrs. Henshaw's house for a half-hour lesson. Margaret Davis had the lesson just before her, and Suzy stared at Margaret's corkscrew curls bouncing up and down to the music. Margaret had been taking lessons for several years, and was much better than Suzy.

Suzy didn't mind the lessons, but she hated to practice. Her mother made her practice for half an hour each day. These practice sessions were generally preceded by a major battle between Suzy and her mother; Suzy always had something else she wanted to do instead. Her mother always won the battle, however, and Suzy found herself at the piano, playing "Mr. Frog is Full of Hops," while her mind wandered to thoughts about how mad she was at her mother. Sometimes, she banged out "MR. FROG IS FULL OF HOPS" to vent her anger and to make sure her mother knew just how mad she really was. She checked the grandfather clock every few minutes to see if her practice time was up yet.

As much as Suzy hated to practice, she loved to perform. Twice a year, Mrs. Henshaw's students gave a recital in the auditorium of Hamilton Elementary School. Suzy wore her best dress and black patent leather shoes to the January recital. Her mother tied her hair back with a red ribbon so it wouldn't fall in her face while she played. Suzy could see her family sitting in the second row while she waited impatiently backstage. Philip was squirming, and Suzy prayed that he wouldn't do anything embarrassing. Margaret Davis' piece seemed to go on forever, but finally it was Suzy's turn. She took a little bow to the audience then sat down at the piano. She stumbled over the part that always gave her trouble, but breezed through the rest of the song. She fantasized that she was a famous concert pianist, on a worldwide tour. The applause made her giddy and convinced her that the piano was her life. But the next day, practicing her finger exercises, the glamor was gone, and she found herself staring at the clock again, willing the minutes away.

The Little House

Julia's birthday was coming up next month, and Matthew decided to build her a wooden house for her dolls. After all, the project would simply be model-making on a grand scale. The house for Julia was built from a kit Matthew had bought at a hobby shop. Matthew followed the directions to put the house together, then added some of his own touches. He cut up popsicle sticks and glued them to the roof for shingles. Mother gave him scraps of material to use for wallpaper and rugs. He cut out a little door and hinged it so it would open and close easily. On the front of the house, over the door, he painted the numbers 2310, which was their address on Chilton Road. The house was painted gray, with a red door. A narrow wooden staircase connected the two floors.

Dad and Matthew made doll house furniture out of wood and clay. They built a wooden fireplace, and Matthew gathered tiny sticks from outside to use as logs. Mom sewed miniature cushions for the sofas and chairs, using a fabric similar to the slipcovers in their living room. She also made wee curtains for the windows.

The night before her birthday, when Julia finally fell asleep, Matthew carried the house up from the basement and put it on the kitchen table, so Julia would see it when she came downstairs for breakfast. She loved the house, and immediately moved her family of dolls into it. The house was special, so special that when Julia became too old to play with dolls, she packed the house away carefully, to save for her own children.

Painting the Little House (1921)   35

Boy Running on Beach (c. 1970)

Vacations

Every summer, the Miller family went to the beach. Mr. Miller packed up the car the night before, filling it with the suitcases and duffle bags full of beach towels and toys, until there wasn't an inch of space left in the trunk. Matthew had trouble falling asleep because he was so excited. After he finally nodded off, he dreamed that he was running on a wide, empty beach, with the ocean lapping over his feet. This was a familiar dream to Matthew because he frequently conjured up pleasant images of himself on the beach to chase away the bad thoughts that sometimes crept into his mind at bedtime.

Very early in the morning, when it was still black outside, Mr. Miller woke up the children and said it was time to hit the road. The children, clutching their stuffed animals, piled into the back seat, arguing about who would sit in the middle.

After breakfast, the highway was more crowded, particularly as they approached the beach town. Over the years, the Miller's had stayed in a number of beach-front cottages, and the children played a game to see who could spot the old cottages first. This year's cottage was a duplex, with one apartment on the first floor and another on the second floor.

''Everybody on the beach in five minutes,'' shouted William, when the last suitcase had been carried in from the car. Their mother would have liked to unpack and organize a little, but the children couldn't wait. They put on their bathing suits and ran toward the ocean, squealing as the waves chased them back to shore.

There were certain traditions that the children looked forward to every year. They always went to the boardwalk at least once, to play skee-ball and ride the little cars that turned upside down. Their father always built ball castles in the sand, and the other children on the beach would ask if they too could have a turn dropping the ball through the castle.

When it was time to go home, Matthew and his mother would stand at the ocean one last time and take a deep breath, to fill their lungs with enough sea air to last until next summer.

The Chair

As far as William was concerned, there was only one comfortable chair in the house. It was an old chair that had belonged to his grandparents. Matthew said he could still remember the chair sitting in the living room of their grandparents' old apartment, but William had no such recollection.

The chair had tattered, brown floral upholstery on it, but Mother had recently covered it with a red slipcover. There was a lot of competition for the chair, not just among the siblings, but between the children and the dog. Charlie apparently agreed that this was the most comfortable chair in the house, for he spent a large part of his time curled up in the chair, with a proprietary look on his face.

For William, the chair was synonymous with reading. He would sit in the old chair, in an impossible position for anyone other than a young child, with his legs hanging over the arms and his body kind of curled up. He would become totally absorbed in his book, and not hear Mother calling that it was time to wash up for dinner.

Sometimes, Charlie was already in the chair and refused to budge. So William developed an alternate reading position on the floor next to the chair. He would take the throw pillow off the sofa and prop it under his head, then stick his legs up in the air and rest them on the chair arm. Charlie would look pathetic, as if William were encroaching on his territory, and would shift position so his head was as far away from William's feet as possible.

When his mother redecorated the living room and threatened to give away the chair, William had the chair moved up to his bedroom, even though it made his room pretty crowded. William knew he had a lot of reading to do to get through school, and he wasn't sure he could do it without the old chair's help.

Teenager Studying (1960)

39

After Hours

In their separate bedrooms, in their separate houses, Matthew and Suzy would wait a little after their mothers and fathers had kissed them goodnight and closed their bedroom doors. Then they would quietly turn on the little lamps next to their beds and read, until their eyes became too droopy to focus on the words any longer.

There was something magical about reading late at night, when all was dark and silent outside. The familiar furnishings of their bedrooms faded into the darkness, and the world of the book became reality.

Matthew loved mysteries and adventure stories. The Hardy Boys were his particular favorites. He stopped at the library frequently to see if they had any on the shelf that he hadn't read yet. Mrs. Martin, the librarian, sometimes held one for him, if she knew he had been looking for it.

Sometimes his mother saw the light through the crack under his door, and told him that he needed to go to sleep or else he would be too tired at school tomorrow. He would turn out the light, but, after he was sure she was gone, would read by the light of the little flashlight he kept on the night table, until he reached the end of the chapter. When his grandparents came to visit, Matthew had to share a room with William. William complained that he couldn't fall asleep with a light on in the room, so Matthew had to wait until William was sound asleep before switching on the light.

Suzy was in the middle of *Little Women*, and was having a hard time putting it down. Her mother had read *Little Women* when she was a girl, and said it was one of her favorites. Unfortunately, her mother had not warned her about the part where Beth died. When Suzy came to the part about Beth, it was well past her bedtime. When her mother peeked into her room to check on her, she found Suzy sitting up in bed with tears streaming down her face. "You should have told me that Beth died," Suzy sobbed, "so I would have been prepared." She had an unsettling night's sleep, with images of Jo, Meg, Amy, and poor Beth swirling around in her dreams.

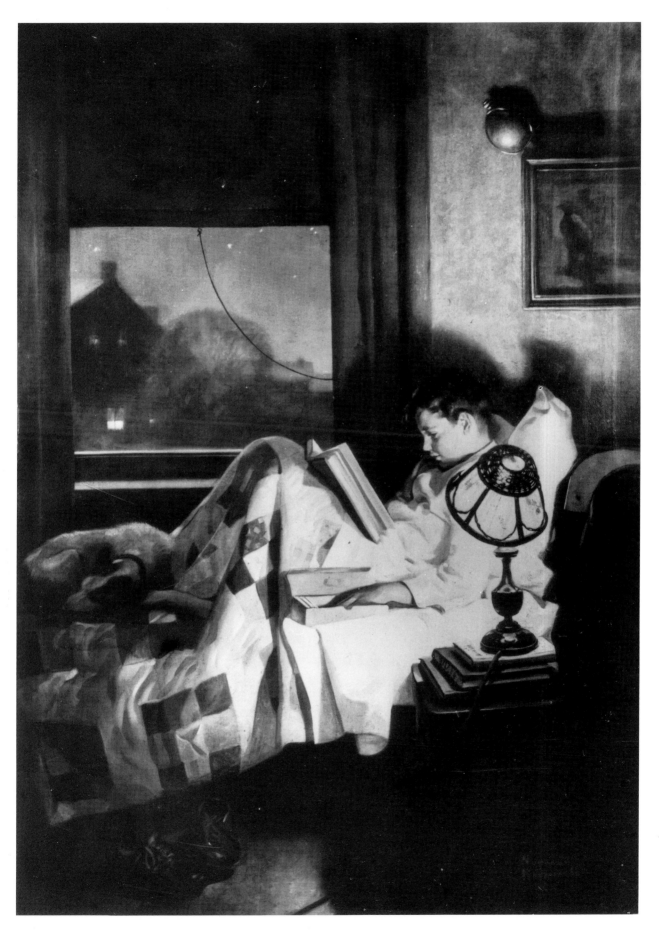

The Omnivorous Reader

When Ned Winter was in second grade, he had to write a report about Abraham Lincoln. "Abe Lincoln was an omnivorous reader," he wrote, having picked up the phrase from a library book about Lincoln. His teacher was impressed, and his parents amused by his choice of words. Ned loved to read and decided that he too was an omnivorous reader. And that is how he described himself throughout his childhood whenever anyone inquired about his interests.

Ned had a secret reading place behind the couch in the living room. He would get up early in the morning, before the rest of the family was up, and read behind the couch. He loved tales of adventure, particularly ones about knights in shining armor saving beautiful princess and going off on quests. In his mind, he became St. George, who saved the beautiful princess from the fire-breathing dragon. The townspeople hailed him as their deliverer after he smote the dragon.

He was a handsome knight, who had saved a lion from drowning. The lion followed him everywhere, and helped him perform good deeds. When the evil knight kidnapped the beautiful princess, the lion, with Ned the Knight on his back, leaped over the moat and the castle walls, and saved the princess.

He was Arthur, armed with a golden sword encrusted with jewels, leading a group of noble knights to victory. Or he was Sir Galahad, on his trusty horse, on a quest to find the Holy Grail. Ned's head was filled with chivalrous adventures, and he bemoaned the fact that it was hard, in these modern times, to find an opportunity to save a village whose crops were being eaten by a wicked dragon.

Marbles

Shooting marbles was a popular pastime for the Chilton Road Gang. With their allowance in their pockets, they'd walk to the five and ten to buy a bag of assorted marbles, or maybe just one large shooter marble. They'd spread their collection of cat's eyes, tiger's eyes, aggies, and shooters out on the sidewalk for the other children to eye and decide which marbles they would try to win.

The children played two versions of marbles. In one version, they'd draw a circle on Marty's driveway with a piece of chalk, or scratch a circle in the dirt with a stick. A group of marbles were placed in the middle of the circle, and the large shooter marbles were used to try to knock the other marbles out of the circle.

The children called the other version of the game, "War." This was played in a large, grassy area. Each child only played with one marble. Whoever hit the other person's marble won. The marbles were thrown a distance into the grass, then the children took turns throwing their marble from wherever it landed to try to hit someone else's marble. There was strategy involved, because if you aimed right for someone else's marble and missed, it might be easy for that person to get you on his next turn.

This version was challenging because it was often difficult to even find the marbles in the grass. But it lent itself to many fights. Since the marbles were often far away, there was frequently a question as to whether your opponent had actually hit your marble, or simply hit a rock near your marble. Since the winner got to take home the loser's marbles, the loser often went home feeling pretty upset.

The boys stuffed their marbles into their book bags in the mornings, because playing marbles was a popular activity on the playground. Sometimes the boys would spread their marbles out on the blacktop and work out trades. Other times they would draw a circle with chalk and play. Fred Pearce, who wasn't very good at athletics, was oddly enough a skillful marble shooter. The boys soon avoided him on the playground, because a game with him meant that they would always lose their favorite marbles.

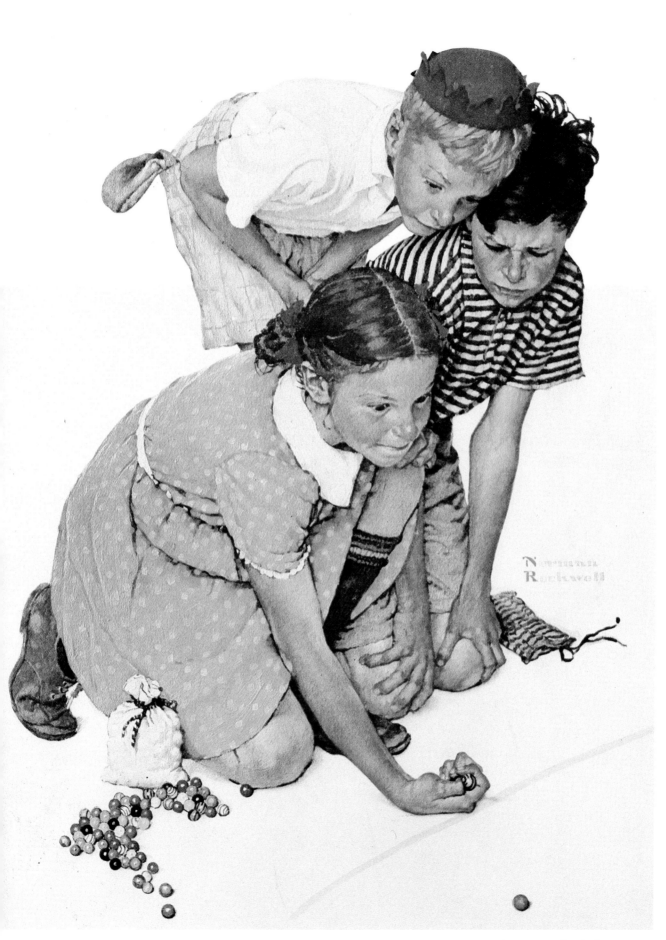

Champion (1939) 45

Girl in Snow with Dog (1916)

The Big Hill

Chilton Road was hilly, and the children could sled either on the road or on the Miller's yard when it snowed. But for really special snowstorms, when schools were closed and businesses were shut down, the children and their families headed for the big hill on Chartley Street, which was widely known as the best sledding hill in town.

The big hill was both scary and exhilarating. There were so many sledders that grassy patches started to appear through the snow. The children tried to avoid the grassy spots, and avoid each other, all while flying at top speed. Everyone loved going down, and hated walking back up. At first, Mom and Dad shared the sleds with the children and pulled them back up. But they tired of sledding and hiking up the hill much faster than the children did, and soon the children were on their own. They tried taking turns pulling each other up the hill, but soon it was each man for himself.

In addition to being tiring, walking up the hill was a bit hair-raising. Children trudged up the hill with their heads down, eyes staring down at the snowy ground. They concentrated on each labored step, saying "I think I can, I think I can," over and over to themselves. With their heads down, they didn't see the oncoming sled until it was almost too late. "Watch out," screamed the child on the sled, unable to control the course of his speeding sled. A collision was avoided by inches.

After sledding, the families piled back in their cars and headed home to change into dry clothes and drink some hot chocolate with marshmallows in it. The cold air made everyone both hungry and sleepy. The children hoped it would snow some more so they wouldn't have to go back to school tomorrow. But they did have to go back to school, and the big hill had to wait for the next big storm.

Sometimes, after the snow had started to melt and only streaks of it remained on the hill, the children drove past the Chartley Street hill and saw some stragglers still sledding, trying to get in a last thrill before the snow was completely gone.

Sunday Mornings

On Sunday mornings the Preston family went to church. Mr. Preston went by himself to the eight o'clock service, because no hymns were sung and the service was shorter. But the rest of the family ate a big breakfast, put on their best clothes, and went to the later service.

Marsha and her sisters always wore their best dresses, straw hats with ribbons on them, and a pair of short, white gloves that were only used on Sundays. All year round, they wore short white socks, folded down at the ankles, and black patent leather shoes; in the winter their knees froze.

The children didn't look forward to church because they didn't like having to sit still and be quiet. Marsha had trouble keeping her mind on the service, but knew to stand up when the other people stood up, and sit down when everyone else sat down.

Marsha cautiously looked around to spot her friends, and gave them small waves when her mother wasn't looking. Her brother Luke crawled under the pews, and once ended up rows and rows in front of the family before Mother realized what he had done. Crawling under the pews was a favorite pastime of the little boys, and it was not surprising to find someone else's child suddenly appear rows in front of where his own family was sitting.

Butch was in the choir, and went to weekly practices as well as to the Sunday service. He was always the one hamming it up, and getting silly with his friends.

Mother and Daughter Singing in Church (1921) 49

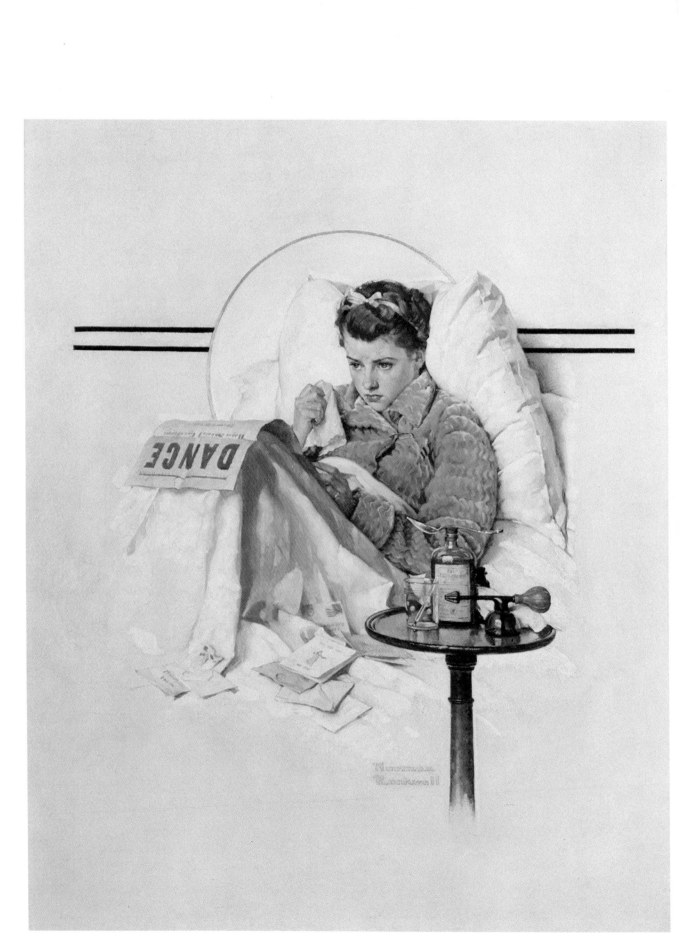

Girl Sick in Bed (1937)

Chapter 2
Sick Days

The Killer Cold

Julia caught a lot of colds, not regular colds like the other kids, but KILLER COLDS. She would have a raw, uncomfortable throat for three days before the cold even got rolling. Julia's mother kept her home from school, sometimes for as long as two weeks, and kept her confined to bed for much of this time. She brought Julia extra pillows and propped her up high on the bed. Next to the bed she arranged a pile of comic books, Nancy Drews, and magazines, and drawing paper and crayons. Occasionally, the family television set was rolled into Julia's room during the day, so that she could watch cartoons, quiz shows and comedy reruns while the other children were at school.

The silver, lidded pitcher, which only came out when someone in the Miller household was ill, was filled with cold orange juice and placed next to the bed, so Julia's mother didn't have to run up and down the stairs each time Julia needed a drink. Meals were served to Julia in bed, on a tray. At dinnertime, she ate her food listening to the muffled voices downstairs at the dinner table. Julia strained to hear what was being discussed, and felt oddly alienated and expendable.

In fact, the oddest part about being sick for Julia was realizing that everyday life went on without her. The family didn't seem to miss her at meals; the children in her class continued working on their science projects despite her absence; and Mrs. Elsnor assigned the parts for the dance recital even though Julia wasn't there. Before dinner, Julia heard the metal of the children's roller skates scraping on the concrete sidewalk. She started to feel a little sorry for herself.

During the time Julia was sick, Joanna stopped by after school to drop off the day's homework. Julia wondered why she still had to do homework when she wasn't allowed to do anything else. William took the completed homework to school with him and dropped it off in Miss Randolph's class.

At bedtime, Julia's mother gave her a spoonful of thick, cherry-flavored cough syrup. Julia loved the smell and taste of the medicine, and the way it felt as it coated her throat. She slept, still propped high on extra pillows, listening to the hissing of the vaporizer.

The Doctor's Office

Annual visits to the doctor were a cause of both excitement and fear for William. Going for a checkup meant that he was another year older, which was exciting because it felt like he was catching up to Matthew. It meant that the nurse would give him a lollipop in the color of his choice when the visit was over.

However, a checkup also meant, in all probability, a shot, and William hated shots. His arm always became red, swollen, and achy afterward. Just looking at a syringe made him feel dizzy with fear. Dr. McGarity taught him a special technique for getting shots. He told William to look away, hold his breath, and count to three; by the time he got to three, the shot would be over. William found this advice to be helpful, although it didn't ease the pain he felt in his arm later. He continued to use this technique well into adulthood.

Dr. McGarity was a young, thin man with black hair and a gentle voice. He had a partner, Dr. Wilton, who was a much older man with gray hair. He saw William sometimes when Dr. McGarity was on vacation, but William didn't like him as much as he liked Dr. McGarity.

The doctor's office had pictures of cars all over the office. Dr. McGarity frequently discussed cars with William during his examination. The waiting room was full of toys for children to play with while they waited, but William's mother said the toys were full of germs and wouldn't let William touch them. He always spent his waiting time reading. There were children's books and magazines in the rack in the corner of the waiting room. William liked the magazines with the hidden pictures page, but it was frustrating because other children always circled the hidden pictures, giving away their location and ruining the fun for the next child.

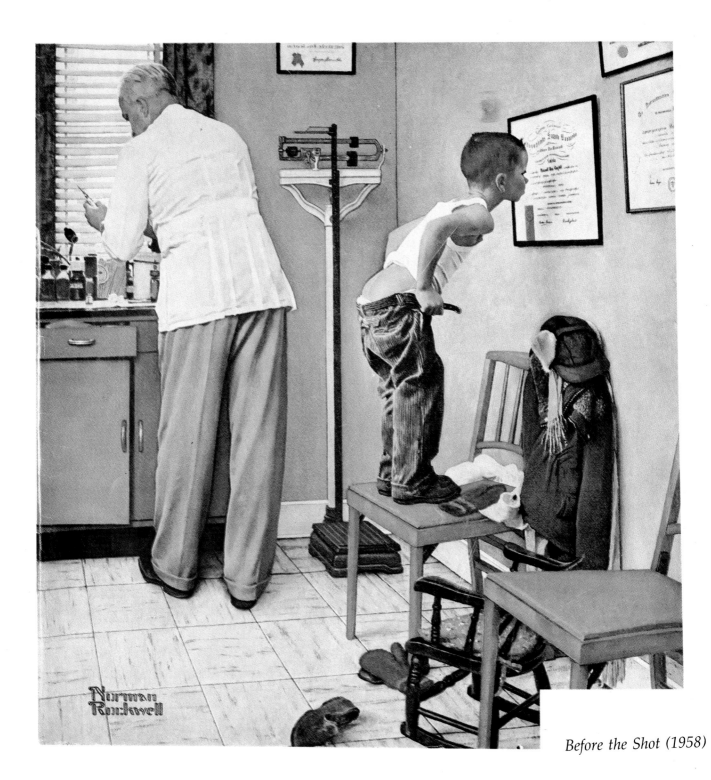

Before the Shot (1958)

When William's name was called, he went back to the examining room, took off his shoes, and stood on the big scale. It was exhilarating to see how much he had grown in a year. Dr. McGarity listened to his chest with a stethoscope, which felt icy cold against his skin. Then the doctor let William listen to his own heartbeat. He always let William take a fistful of tongue depressors home, which his mother later found lying all around the house and threw out.

After checkups, William and his mother would go to Reese's drugstore and buy ice cream sodas. His mother always ordered vanilla ice cream with chocolate soda, but William was a purist, at least where chocolate was concerned, and went for chocolate ice cream in the chocolate soda.

The Home Visit

When Julia was four years old, she had the chicken pox and measles at the same time. When her mother came in to her room, Julia turned her face to the wall and said, "Please go away and let me suffer alone." This rattled Mrs. Miller so much that she immediately went to call the doctor, and implored him to come over to examine Julia as soon as possible.

Dr. Wilton came to their house, carrying his black bag, that afternoon, after his appointments for the day were completed. He had never seen a case of the measles and chicken pox at the same time, and was intrigued. He didn't charge for the visit, because Julia had made medical history, at least as far as he knew. Years later, Julia's mother saw an article on the front page of the newspaper about a child who had measles and chicken pox at the same time. She was indignant that the paper made such a big deal about it because, after all, Julia had done that ages ago.

Whenever the children were really sick, Dr. McGarity or Dr. Wilton came to the house. They always carried a black bag, stuffed with an incredible number of medical instruments and medications. They were very friendly and jocular during these visits, but there was a formality about them too, which seemed out of place with the informality of the Miller household.

After the doctor finished examining the sick child, Mrs. Miller always offered him a cup of tea and some cookies. Sometimes he declined, saying that he had other calls to make. But other times, he took her up on the offer and stayed downstairs chitchatting and gossiping for quite a while. The next day, he always called on the telephone to "see how his patient was," and to thank Mrs. Miller for her hospitality.

The Eye Doctor

Marty sat in the next-to-last row of seats in the classroom. He wasn't doing very well on tests, even though he had never had trouble with schoolwork before. His teacher, Mrs. Shaw, afraid that Marty wasn't paying attention in class, moved him to the front row. Marty's work improved dramatically. Mrs. Shaw, sensing that something was amiss, asked Marty to stand near the back of the room and read what was written on the board. He couldn't do it—it turned out that Marty needed glasses.

Marty's mother took him to Dr. Norton, where his eyesight was tested in a big room. Dr. Norton asked Marty to read the eye chart, then he asked him to look at red and green lights. A big contraption was put against Marty's face, and Dr. Norton inserted different lenses into it. "Does this one look better?" asked Dr. Norton. "Or this one?" he queried as he continued to switch lenses. Marty was getting very confused, because it was hard to tell the difference between some of the lenses. He wondered if he should say, "Yes, this one is better," just to make Dr. Norton happy. Finally, he agreed that one lens *might* look better than the others, and Dr. Norton nodded sagely as if he knew all along that Marty would pick that one.

Next, Dr. Norton put drops in Marty's eyes and told him to sit in the waiting room for a little while. Marty picked up the magazine he had been looking at earlier, and started reading the article detailing new theories about whether dinosaurs were cold-blooded or warm-blooded. Soon, his eyes became blurry and he could no longer read. He went to the bathroom and stared at his reflection in the mirror—his pupils looked very large and very black.

Dr. Norton handed him a paper with a prescription for glasses. Marty and his mother drove to the opticians that Marty's dad had always used. His mother picked out brown frames that were not as dashing as Marty would have liked.

When he went to pick up the glasses, the opticians had to heat up the frames and bend them to fit his face just right. The glasses felt funny against Marty's head and on his nose. The glasses looked strange to him, although later he became so used to wearing the glasses that his face started looking strange without them.

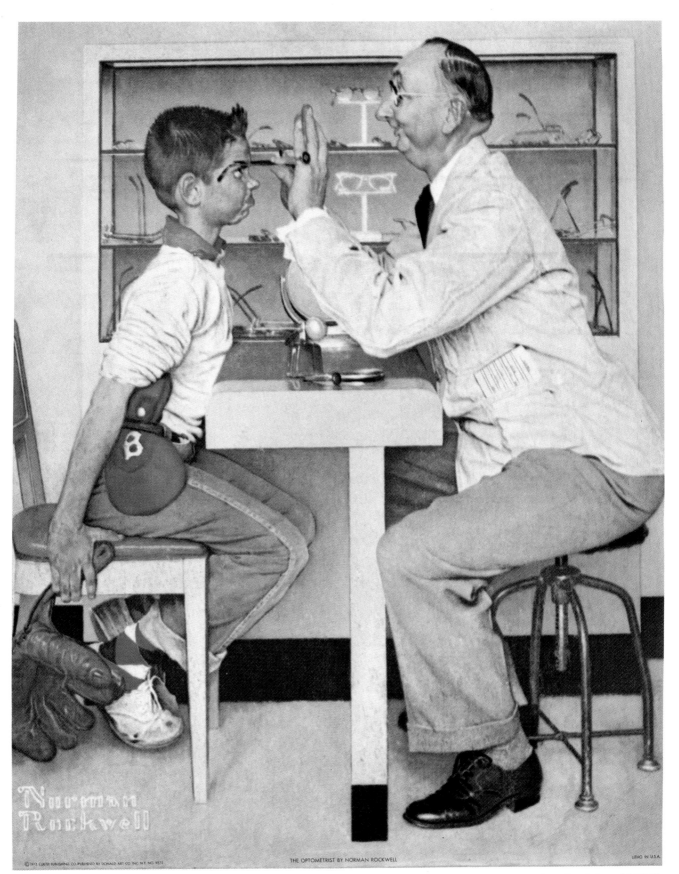

The Optician (1956)

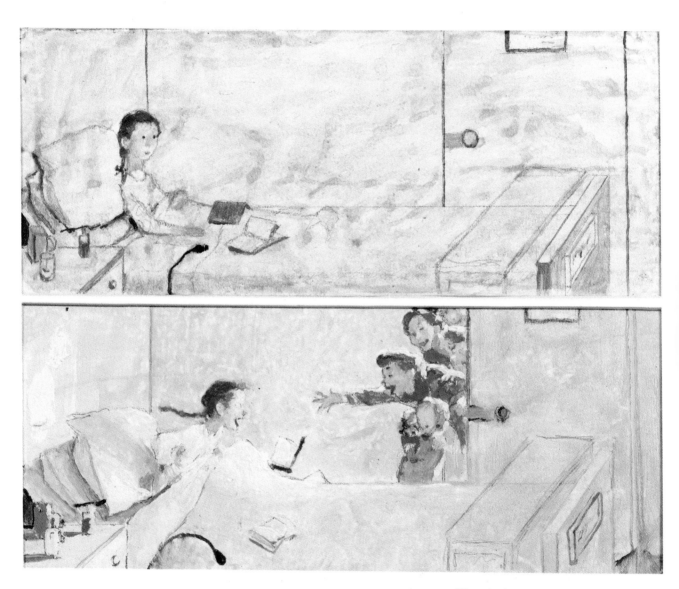

Hospital Room (Date Unknown)

60

The Hospital Visit

The big news on Chilton Road was that Marsha Preston was in the hospital having her tonsils taken out. She and her mother went to the hospital first thing in the morning, but ended up sitting in the waiting room a long time, waiting to register. Mrs. Preston began reading a book to a nervous Marsha. They got halfway through it before Marsha's name was finally called. She was led upstairs to the children's ward, and shown into a room with two beds. The other bed was already occupied by a girl named Marilee, who was a couple years younger than Marsha and who was also getting her tonsils out that day. The nurse showed Marsha and Marilee a room down the hall, which was filled with toys and several other children. She said they could play there until they were called.

Marsha was called back to the room and given a shot to make her sleepy. Then she was placed on a stretcher and wheeled down to the operating room. Her mother walked beside the stretcher, but had to stop at the door of the operating room, because she wasn't allowed inside. Marsha vaguely remembered a mask coming down over her face; then, the next thing she knew, she was waking up with an incredibly sore throat. Her mother spent the night in a large chair next to the bed, and the other Preston children were allowed in briefly to see her. Marilee cried and drank sodas all night, and by morning had worked herself into a fever and was not allowed to go home when Marsha did. This made her cry even more.

At home, Marsha was fed popsicles, ice cream, popsicles, and ice cream. Friends kept sending her more and more ice cream—fancy ones cut in slices, decorated with flowers, and individually wrapped in white paper. Marsha, who used to love ice cream, began to gag at the sight of it. The fancy ice creams were given to the other Preston kids who, unlike Marsha, had not reached their ice cream saturation point yet.

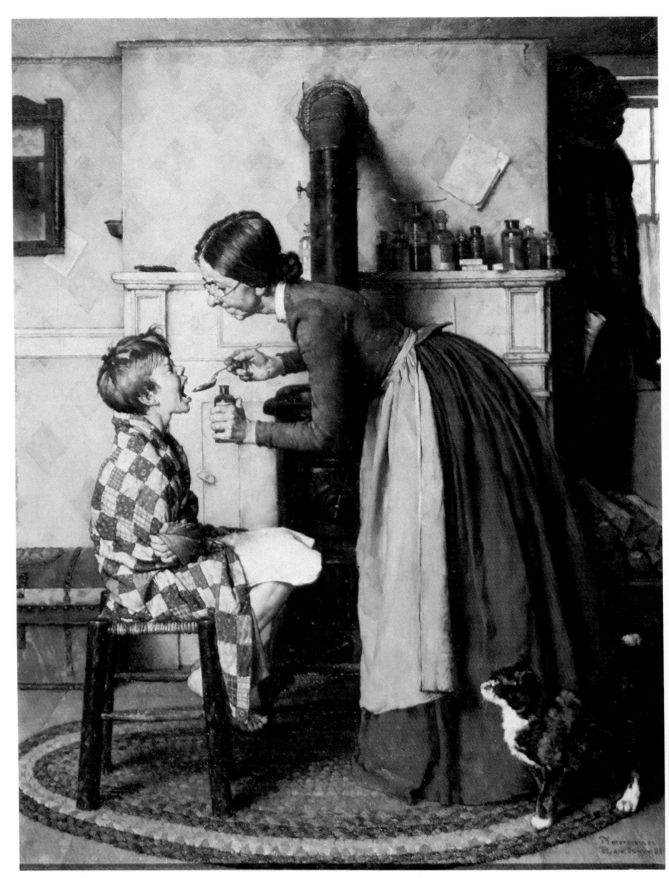

Spring Tonic (1936)

The Medicine

It was bad enough getting sick, and not being able to go to the circus, or play outside with the gang; but to add insult to injury, there was THE MEDICINE. The medicine that the children were given when they were sick was frequently worse than the sickness itself.

There wasn't really just one dreaded medication, but a whole arsenal of disgusting tasting liquids. There was the white, chalky stuff (as in "Aw, Mom, not *that* awful stuff"); the oily stuff; the cherry stuff that was so thick it stuck in the childrens' throats; the pink stuff that smelled like bubble gum but tasted like turpentine.

The children had different ways of handling the difficult medicine situation, which reflected their different personalities. Philip used to run and hide in the closet, hoping his mother wouldn't find him until he was healthy again. William held his nose, closed his eyes, and swallowed quickly. Marty kept the medicine in one hand and a glass of water in the other, and washed down the medicine with the water so quickly that his mother was always afraid he would choke. Julia preferred a martyr approach—she just sat in a resigned manner and cooperated completely. By doing this, she could spend the rest of the day pointing out how good she was about taking *her* medicine, not like some other children she knew.

Mrs. Johnson, the school nurse, gave Matthew some medicine-taking advice that proved to be very helpful. Her suggestion was that, prior to taking a nasty-tasting liquid, he should suck on an ice cube. This would anesthetize his taste buds and make the medicine more palatable. This technique did nothing to alleviate the unpleasant thick, oily, or chalky textures of the medicines, but definitely helped the taste problem, which was, after all, half of the battle.

Comforts

William's mother always said, "The illness just has to run its course." This may have been true, but there were comforts that could be provided to help pave the way to better health.

First, there was the rub down. When the children had a cold, their mothers rubbed their chests with vapor rub, then placed a really hot washcloth on top. The entire house smelled unpleasantly of vapor rub, but the children believed they could actually feel the warmth penetrating their chests and breaking up the congestion. When they had a high fever, their mothers would rub the children all over with witch hazel. This technique was also used when they got overheated in the summer. The rub down definitely had certain psychological benefits—it felt good, therefore it must be working.

Another comfort to the children during the miseries of illness was having a nest for themselves, either on their bed, their parents' bed, or on a favorite chair or sofa. Building a nest involved stocking the adjacent area with necessities such as tissue paper, comic books, drinks, snacks, and luxuries such as extra pillows, favorite comforters, and flannel bathrobes. This way it was possible to be both miserable and cozy at the same time.

A pet was sometimes a comfort to the sick child. Charlie always curled up with Matthew on the big chair in the living room. Stuffed animals that were ignored the rest of the year developed new importance during illnesses, as did old tattered blankets.

Boy and Dog Snuggled in Blanket (c. 1925)

Father and Son Playing Checkers (1958)

Chapter 3
Family Rituals

Playing Games

On weekend nights, after dinner, the Winter family sat around the kitchen table and played games. They played board games and card games. Sometimes they divided into teams, and sometimes it was each man for himself.

Philip loved family game times. He was good at games of logic, and unusually lucky at games of chance. Suzy, however, dreaded game times. She tried to get out of playing, but ran out of excuses eventually. Her problem was that she just wasn't lucky. If doubles were needed to start moving her pawn toward the finish, the dice wouldn't cooperate. The rest of the family would be halfway around the board before doubles finally came up and Suzy could get started. She spent the evening fighting back tears of frustration, and wishing she were somewhere else. She wasn't much better at games of logic, and Philip was constantly pointing out how stupid her move had been.

Family game nights were a time of togetherness and of shared interests, and a time of battles and bruised egos. In short, they were in many ways a microcosm of family life in general.

Father Reading to Daughter (1953)

Reading Time

In virtually every household on Chilton Road reading was usually the last step in the bedtime routine, except for goodnight kisses and prayers.

Julia loved reading time because it was a special time with Dad. He would still be wearing his daytime clothes, and would sit in the chair in the living room with Julia on his lap. She would pick the book she wanted read that night. Sometimes her father read to her, sometimes she read to her father, and sometimes they alternated reading. Sometimes Julia became especially fond of a certain book and picked it over and over again for weeks. Her father would say, "Not this book again," and read in a weary, resigned voice. After trips to the library, when Julia came home with a stack of books, her father agreed to read more than one book, because Julia was so excited and couldn't wait to read all the new books.

Sometimes, she and her father would read long books, a chapter a night. If she had no school the next day, her father would read two or even three chapters, letting Julia stay up later than usual.

Once Julia became intrigued by wolves and wanted to read *Peter and the Wolf* every night. The book remained next to her bed at night so that she could find it easily the next evening. Then suddenly she became afraid of wolves. The wolf on the cover of the book seemed to glow in the dark and jump off the page at her. She made her father hide the book somewhere in the attic, so the wolf couldn't get her. Months later, she asked her father to bring the book down to read to her, then store it back in the attic at night.

Reading Aloud

Marsha only saw her grandparents a couple times a year. They lived in a different state, a long car drive away. Once or twice a year, Marsha's family piled into the family station wagon and drove up to visit them. At Christmas time, her grandparents came to Marsha's house, because the children were afraid that Santa wouldn't find them if they weren't on Chilton Road.

The year Marsha learned to read, she couldn't wait for her grandparents' visit. She had been practicing on several books, reading aloud to herself in her room every night. She intended to read a different book to her grandparents each night they were here.

Her *piece de resistance* was *The Night Before Christmas*. She had just given a triumphant reading of the poem to her kindergarten class, and planned to dazzle her grandparents with her rendition on Christmas Eve. She tended to stumble over the part that said, "His droll little mouth was drawn up like a bow, And the beard on his chin was as white as the snow. The stump of a pipe he held tight in his teeth, And the smoke, it encircled his head like a wreath." Marsha practiced that part over and over until she was sure it was perfect.

On Christmas Eve, she brought the book down and told everyone to please be quiet because she was going to read. Her grandfather sat right next to her, because he was a little hard of hearing and didn't want to miss any of the words. Marsha read perfectly, and when she had finished shouting out "Happy Christmas to all, and to all a good night," the whole family applauded. It became a tradition for Marsha to bring out *The Night Before Christmas* and read it to the family every Christmas Eve. Hearing her voice, the family was always reminded of the five-year-old Marsha, just learning to read.

The Reading Hour (1922)

Bath Time

Bath time was a mixed blessing in the Miller household. Julia hated to be bathed, mainly because she hated having her hair washed. The shampoo, which was supposed to be tearless, stung her eyes. Her hair was always tangled, and after a shampoo her mother spent a long, painful time trying to comb out the tangles. Julia screamed so loud that Mrs. Miller was sure everyone on Chilton Street must know it was Julia's bath time.

William and Matthew, on the other hand, loved bath time. They also loved puddles, swimming, mudholes—anything that was remotely wet. Mrs. Miller always told the story about how, when Matthew was only four months old, he went to the hospital to have a hernia operation. She was not allowed to feed him after midnight, and when he awoke at four o'clock in the morning for his usual feeding, she didn't know how to stop his screaming. Down the hall from Matthew's hospital room was a bathroom, with a huge, deep, old-fashioned porcelain tub. After getting the nurse's permission, Mrs. Miller gave Matthew an early morning bath, which delighted him so much that he actually stopped crying.

William and Matthew took their baths together, which meant that the tub was pretty crowded, considering the number of bath toys they brought in with them. Julia took her dolls into the tub and bathed them too. After the children got out of the tub, their mother had to fish around in the cloudy water to make sure there were no small toys that might go down the drain. Sometimes, after the water drained, the toys were left in the empty tub to dry out, which annoyed Mr. Miller when he stepped in the tub to take his morning shower.

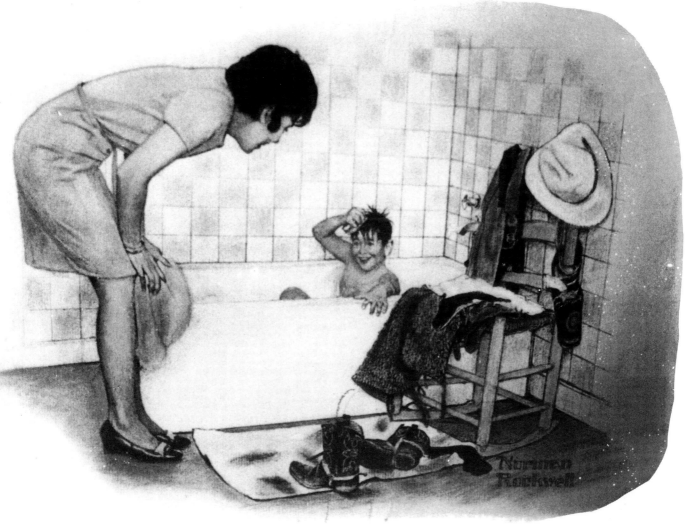

Boy Bathing (c. 1970)

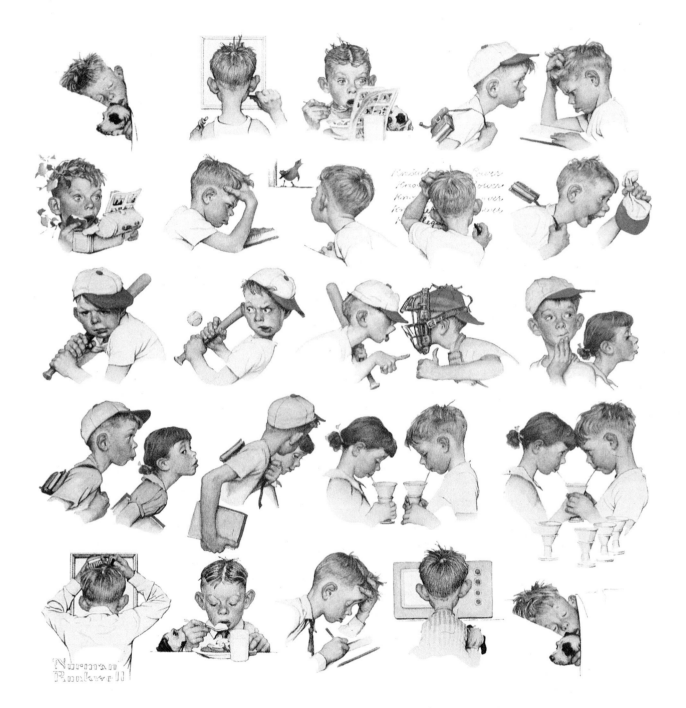

Day in the Life of a Little Boy (1952)

74

Toweling Off

When William and Matthew were small, their parents would lift them from the bathtub and wrap their dripping bodies in a towel. The towel would cover their entire body, and form a protective house for them to hide in. As they grew, the towel covered less and less of their bodies, much to their chagrin. They begged their mother for two towels, one to cover the upper part of their body and one to cover the bottom half. They loved being swathed in towels, and put off getting into their pajamas as long as possible.

William loved his father to wrap the towel around him and tuck in the edges, so that it fit him like a sarong. He would run around the house in his "towel robe" as the towel slipped farther and farther down toward his feet. When the towel hit the floor, William would implore his father to fasten it again up under his arms.

Julia had a pink towel with a satin ballet slipper on it that Aunt Betty had given her for her birthday. She loved the towel and threw a tantrum when it was in the laundry and her mother tried to dry her with the blue towels the rest of the household used. One night, Julia's mother found her asleep in bed, snuggling up to the pink towel, which was slightly damp. Her mother gently removed the towel and hung it back up on the rack in the bathroom, and Julia didn't seem to remember anything about it when she woke up in the morning.

Sleeping Children

Each child in the Winter household had a different way of going to sleep. Suzy needed her mother to sit on the bed next to her for a few minutes, while Suzy stroked her arms and touched her face. After Suzy fell asleep, her mother smoothed out the covers and tiptoed out of the room.

Philip piled his bed high with everything imaginable: mounds of stuffed animals, including the huge bear that he had won at the beach, afghans that his grandmother had crocheted, throw pillows which he had spirited out of his mother's room, and bolsters from the day bed. There was barely room in the bed for Philip, who curled up in a ball in the corner of the bed. He always gave his mother a big bear hug and then asked to be tucked in. Tucking in a boy who has mountains of objects in bed with him was not an easy feat. Ten or fifteen minutes after she turned out Philip's light, Philip always called for help in a pathetic voice. When his mother entered the room, she could see that the bed was a disaster area. The covers were not only untucked but had been yanked from under the mattress with such force that they were lying willy-nilly across the bed. The mound of animals and pillows had somehow gotten taller, if possible, and it was obvious to any rational human being that no person would be able to sleep under such conditions. Mrs. Winter took half of the objects off the bed and piled them neatly on the floor. She then straightened the covers, tucked Philip in again, and sternly told him to go to sleep.

Ned was at an age where he just barely put up with his mother's goodnight kiss, and was anxious for her to close his door and leave him alone. Then he turned on the small light next to his bed and read until he fell asleep.

Before Mr. and Mrs. Winter went to sleep themselves, they checked on the children. Mrs. Winter pulled up the covers that Suzy had kicked off in her sleep. She then removed the remaining pillows and animals from Philip's bed, and turned off the light in Ned's room, placing his book on his night table carefully so as not to lose his place.

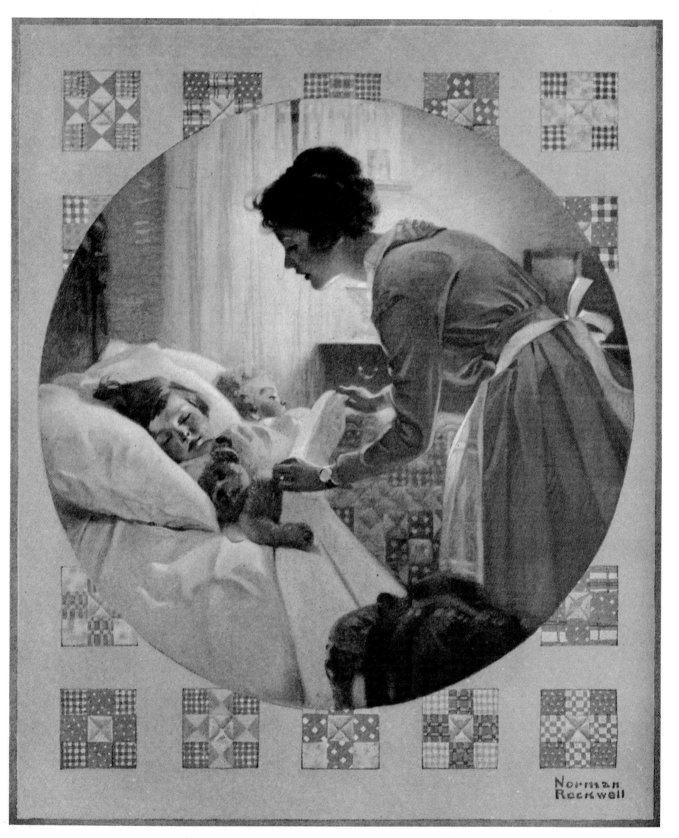

Mother Tucking Children into Bed (1921)

The Toy Maker (1920)

Chapter 4
Grandparents

The Toy Maker

Matthew's grandfather had always been good at making things out of wood. He made the bed Matthew slept in, the coffee table in the living room, and the huge grandfather clock in his own house. But when he was younger, he didn't have much time for woodworking. For forty years he took the commuter train into the city and arrived home in the evenings exhausted and cranky.

After he retired, the first thing Grandfather did was organize his workshop. He built a new, long workbench in the middle of the basement, and hung all his tools on the walls. He sorted his nails, screws, nuts, and bolts, and collected coffee cans in which to keep assorted wires and related paraphernalia.

Soon a heavy package arrived at Matthew's house. For Matthew, Grandfather had filled a large box with handmade wooden blocks—rectangle, square, and cylindrical blocks. Grandfather had sanded the blocks until they were very, very smooth. For William, Grandfather had made a wooden fire truck, with a little ladder that could be taken on and off the truck. For Julia, there was a wooden cradle for her favorite doll. It was made out of beautiful maple, and Grandfather had stenciled hearts and flowers on the sides of the cradle.

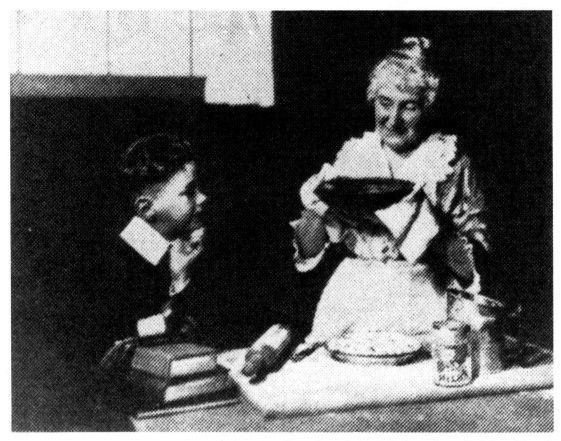

Grandmother and Grandson Baking Pies (1920)

Grandmother's House

Before he moved to Chilton Road, Marty's family lived in his grandmother's house, the same one she had shared with Marty's grandfather when he was alive. There were certain things Marty remembered about his grandmother's house. For one thing, the family always ate in the dining room, even though the kitchen was easily large enough for a table to fit. Meals were very formal, and very plentiful. His grandmother considered it to be a personal insult if Marty didn't help himself to seconds or thirds.

Another unusual thing about his grandmother's house was that it had two big stone tubs in the basement. In the summer, Marty and his cousin took baths in the large tubs. There were drains on the basement floor, so Marty could splash all he wanted and it didn't matter if the floor got wet. When the weather was cold, he wasn't allowed to bathe in the basement, for fear that he might catch a chill.

But the thing Marty remembered most about living in his grandmother's house was that his grandmother always seemed to be baking. Her specialty was chocolate cake. Marty would watch her make the batter, from scratch of course, and wait for his chance to lick the bowl. It seemed to him that his grandmother did an inordinate amount of beating—she'd beat and beat the batter, then beat and beat the icing. In fact, Marty used to think that if she continued to beat any longer, her arm might fall off.

She was also an excellent pie baker. She showed Marty how to roll out the crust until it was very thin, and told him tips passed on by her own mother about how to make the flakiest crust.

When Marty's family moved to Chilton Road, his grandmother moved with them. She still baked cakes and pies for the family. But she no longer spent as much time in the kitchen. She regarded it as Marty's mother's domain now, rather than her's.

A Death in the Family

Suzy was in second grade when her grandfather died. Her father came inside the school, to meet Suzy and Philip before they started walking home. Suzy's grandfather was in the hospital for a couple weeks the previous month, when he had suffered a heart attack. But Suzy thought her grandfather had been feeling better now. However, he suffered another heart attack, this one fatal.

Suzy's father drove them to their cousin Mary's house to stay for a few days. Ned had gone home with a friend and would join them later. Suzy usually loved going to Mary's house because she had a large playroom, with lots of chairs in it. Suzy and Mary lined up the chairs in rows to play school, or sometimes, at Philip's request, to play train.

All the children were upset about their grandfather's death, but Suzy was the most upset. She had a special relationship with her grandfather; because she was the only girl in the family, he doted on her. He was always playful and full of fun. Sometimes he would darken the room, except for one lamp, which he pointed toward the wall. The children sat facing the wall, while Grandfather made animal shadows with his hands. He tried to show Suzy how to make the animals, but she could never get her hands positioned exactly right.

Their grandfather also loved to make up rhymes. While he was in the hospital the first time, he wrote poems about each of the children, which he gave to them when they came to visit. He also loved tongue twisters. "I scream, you scream, we all scream for ice cream," or "she sells sea shells down by the seashore," always reminded Suzy of her grandfather.

After he died, Suzy listened to her grandfather's favorite songs on the record player and talked to him up in the sky. He was the first important person in her life to have died, and he left her with many memories that she carried with her throughout her life.

The Children's Hour (1922)

Grandfather's Bargain (1915)

Tricks and Treats

When the Preston children visited their grandparents, they knew just what to expect. They'd open the back door of their grandparent's house and shout "Boo!" as loudly as possible. Their grandfather would jump, pretending to be scared.

If it was a nice day, their grandfather would slip the children a dollar each, and walk with them to the corner store to buy candy. He'd show off his grandchildren to Mr. Moore, the storekeeper, and to any neighbors they happened to meet along the way.

Their grandmother, meanwhile, had prepared a feast consisting of all the children's favorite foods, or at least the foods that had been their favorite at the time of the last visit. It was hard to keep up with favorite foods, particularly with Robert, who could love something one week and detest it the next. Marsha could tell that her grandmother's feelings were a bit hurt when Robert would say, "Yuck, I hate spaghetti," after Grandmother had gone to all the trouble of making it, thinking it was his favorite dish.

After dinner, their grandfather would suddenly look at one of the children and say, "What's that sticking out of your ear?" "I don't know," replied the child, straining in vain to get a view of his ear. At that, their grandfather would walk over and pull a nickel out of the ear. At various times during the visit, he would pull money out of the other children's ears, or noses, or hair.

Their grandfather kept his cigars in a shiny silver cigar box with gold trim. The children took turns retrieving cigars for him, because the one who brought the cigar to their grandfather got to keep the paper ring that went around it.

By the time their parents came to take them home, the children were loaded down with coins, cigar rings, small toys, and a tin of their favorite cookies, which Grandma had baked. Favorite foods might change from week to week, but not favorite cookies.

Wanderlust

When Marty was little, he would sit on a tiny stool in front of his other grandfather and listen to tales of faraway places. His grandfather had been an adventurer in his youth. He had sailed large ships across the ocean, and had even made his living as a sailmaker at one time. He had worked in the silver mines in Mexico during the time of Pancho Villa, when Mexico was fighting for its independence. When he settled down and married Marty's grandmother, he decided not to ever buy a house or a car, but to use his money instead to travel.

Marty's grandfather and grandmother traveled abroad at least once a year until they tired of it. When they returned from a trip, Marty and his cousins would gather in the sunroom of their grandparents' apartment to see what treasures they had brought back for the children this time. Sometimes they brought back coins, gold square coins and silver coins with holes in the middle. The girls always got dolls— Japanese dolls wearing rich purple kimonos with tiny combs in their hair, Spanish flamenco dancers carrying tiny castanets in their hands. Marty also received wood carvings, boxes, silk kimonos, Swiss walking sticks, maracas, and puppets. He was never at a loss for things to take to school for show and tell.

When his grandparents traveled, they sent him postcards with wonderful stamps on them. Marty's mother bought him a leather-bound photo album, in which he mounted his postcard collection. Sometimes his grandfather sent him long letters, describing a volcano eruption he had just seen, or some other experience that he thought Marty would find particularly interesting. Marty loved to check the return address on his grandfather's letters. It always said something like, "in transit, the Panama Canal."

In first grade, Marty's teacher asked the members of the class what things they wanted to do when they grew up. Marty said, "I want to see the whole wide world."

Sea Captain with Young Boy (c. 1925)

Boy with Puppies (1922)

Chapter 5
A Child's Best Friend

The Puppy

The puppy became part of the Winter household unexpectedly. Uncle Jack was suddenly transferred to the West coast, and his beagle puppy was suddenly transferred to Suzy, Philip, and Ned. The puppy's name was Ozzie, and he was black, with a white face and paws. The children were delighted with Ozzie, although their parents were less thrilled.

Mrs. Winter said the puppy had to stay in the kitchen until he was completely trained. Uncle Jack had paper-trained Ozzie, but had gotten no farther. Mr. Winter built a gate across the kitchen door, so Ozzie couldn't go wandering into the dining and living rooms.

The first night, Ozzie whimpered all night. Philip finally took a sleeping bag down to the kitchen and slept on the floor with the puppy, which helped quiet him down. The next day, the children took a big box, turned it on its side, and padded it with an old quilt. Philip put his unwashed undershirt in the box, and Ned put in the red socks that Aunt Elizabeth had given him, which he had always hated. Suzy put in a travel alarm clock, which had such a loud tick that Mrs. Winter kept hiding it under pillows to muffle the sound. Suzy had read in a book that the ticking of a clock was comforting to puppies.

Ozzie seemed to like his new home, and didn't cry at all the next night. He did, however, wake up *very* early. Mrs. Winter said that it was like having a baby again. The children knew when Ozzie woke up because they could hear his tail thumping against the refrigerator as he stood at the gate, waiting for one of them to come play. The children took turns going down to the kitchen at the crack of dawn to play with Ozzie and put him outside in the ivy "to do his business." After he was trained, Ozzie was allowed to wander wherever he wanted in the house. He spent his nights sprawled out on Philip's bed, while Philip curled up in the little space left.

Jasper

Mr. and Mrs. Miller had bought Charlie before the children were born. Although Charlie appeared to be fond of the children, and was certainly very protective of them, Matthew was always aware that Charlie belonged to his parents rather than to him. It was their bed Charlie slept near, and it was them he went to for comfort when he was scared by thunder or firecrackers.

Jennie lived around the corner on Ranchleigh Road. She was fourteen years old, and frequently babysat for Matthew, William, and Julia. One night when she was babysitting, Jennie told the children that her dog, Claire, was going to have puppies. She promised that they could come play with the puppies whenever they wanted.

Matthew was excited; he wasn't born when Charlie was a puppy, and when he saw friends' puppies, they were usually at least a couple months old. He had never seen a newborn puppy before.

There were eight puppies in Claire's litter, six males and two females. Most of the puppies were white like Claire, with patches of black on their faces and ears. One puppy was brown with hardly any white on him at all. Matthew, William, and Julia couldn't believe how tiny the puppies were.

Several times a week, after school, Matthew walked to Jennie's house to play with the puppies. He sat on the floor and the puppies jumped all over him, licking his face and nipping his ear. One puppy, named Jasper, spent the most time with Matthew. Jasper stood on Matthew's lap while he licked his face, or sometimes curled up next to Matthew and chewed his sneakers. Matthew loved all the puppies, but he loved Jasper best.

When the puppies were about seven weeks old, Jennie's family began looking for homes for them. Little Joe was the first to go, then Ashley. One day, Jennie said they had found a home for Jasper, and that this would be his last week at her house. Matthew was heartbroken and held Jasper so tightly the puppy tried to squirm out of his arms.

The day Jasper left, Matthew moped outside by the big oak tree. He didn't want to come in when his mother called. But when he got inside, there was Jasper sitting in a box on the kitchen floor! "I thought someone bought him," exclaimed Matthew. "Someone did," said his father, "we did." So Jasper became Matthew's pal and inseparable companion, and for months Matthew walked around in chewed-up sneakers.

The Medicine

Matthew knew Jasper was sick when he wouldn't eat his food, and showed no interest in the piece of cheese Matthew dangled in front of his face. He just stayed huddled up in his box, looking pathetic. Matthew felt sorry for the dog, who obviously felt miserable, but he also felt sorry for himself. He knew it was his job to force Jasper to take whatever medicine the veterinarian prescribed.

Getting Jasper to take medicine was a difficult job, requiring both ingenuity and perseverance. Matthew took Jasper's pills and padded them with ground beef. Jasper somehow managed to eat every shred of beef, while still leaving the pill intact, sitting in the middle of his dog dish. Next Matthew tried holding Jasper's mouth open and shoving the pill down his throat. This technique appeared to be successful, until Matthew spotted the pill on the floor a few minutes later. Somehow Jasper had managed to spit out the pill without Matthew seeing or hearing a thing. Matthew held open Jasper's mouth and shoved the pill back in again. This time, he watched Jasper like a hawk, daring him to spit up the pill. No pill reappeared, and the deed appeared done. Matthew held out a dog biscuit to Jasper, to congratulate him for taking the pill, but as Jasper opened his mouth to devour the biscuit, out popped the pill. He had been storing it in his mouth, waiting for a chance to ditch it.

Liquids were not much easier to dispense. If Matthew poured the liquid down Jasper's throat, he choked and spit up half the medicine. Matthew tried mixing the medicine with chicken soup, or using it as a gravy for turkey scraps, which were Jasper's favorite, but Jasper wasn't fooled. Matthew remembered hearing that if you brushed medicine on cat's paws, the cat would lick off the medicine. This technique apparently didn't work on puppies, since Jasper simply ran away through the house, leaving white medicine paw prints in every room.

Somehow Jasper got better despite wasting most of his medicine, and Matthew suspected that Jasper even felt invigorated after waging his successful battles against the medicine.

Sick Puppy (1923)   93

A Visit to the Vet

It was Philip's job to take Ozzie to the vet when he needed shots. It upset Suzy too much to see Ozzie terrified, and Ned was too busy these days. The "animal hospital" was at the bottom of the hill, near school, and Philip walked Ozzie there on a leash. Ozzie was excited to go on a walk, but when they crossed Smith Avenue and headed toward the vet's, he sat down and refused to budge. Philip had to pick him up and carry him into the waiting room.

The receptionist pulled out Ozzie's card, which was filed under the name "Ozzie Winter." There were several other dogs already waiting to see the doctor. Philip sat down, with a shivering Ozzie on his lap.

Each dog in the waiting room had a distinct personality. There was one shivering (Ozzie), one whimpering, one howling, one quiet but despondent-looking, and one cowering against his owner. There was one trying to drag his owner to the door to escape. And there was one big, shaggy dog, who actually seemed happy to be there. He bounded over to the other animals, appearing to relish this opportunity to see some buddies.

Once Philip sat next to a man with a parrot, who told Philip that the parrot had a cold. He showed Philip how to hold out his fingers, and let the parrot wrap his feet around them, but Philip didn't like the way it felt. The parrot squawked at Ozzie, sending him scrambling under the chair.

Boy in Veterinarian's Office (1952)

Boys Bathing Dog (c. 1920)

Charlie's Bath Time

Charlie instinctively knew when it was bath time. Matthew and his father surreptitiously gathered the shampoo, towels, and brush together, and tried to lure Charlie into the yard with a tennis ball. Charlie, sensing a trap, ran to the far end of the back yard, turned over on his back, and refused to move. When the wash basin appeared, Charlie was sure of their treachery and turned his body into sixty pounds of dead weight. William, Matthew, and their father dragged that one dog to the tub and lifted him in.

It was impossible to bathe Charlie without getting drenched. Charlie had the philosophy that if he had to suffer, he'd bring everyone down with him. Father's job was to hold the squirming Charlie so he wouldn't jump out of the tub, while William's was to hose him with water, and Matthew's to lather him with shampoo. Without his collar on, Charlie was slippery and hard to hold. He always managed to escape before the bath was finished, and would take off across the yard, his hair full of suds, with William and Matthew chasing him.

He was eventually returned to the tub and rinsed off. The first thing Charlie did when removed from the tub was shake the water off, all over Matthew, William, and Father. Next, he ran to the only spot in the yard that didn't have much grass, and rolled over and over in the dirt. This way, he dried himself off and got himself back to his original state of dirtiness. Father, wet and cranky by now, refused to clean off Charlie again. The boys tried to brush the dirt out, and Charlie, looking little better than before the cleaning process, was kept outside until his fur was completely dry.

The Doll Doctor

When Philip was born, Suzy was given a beautiful new doll with a soft body and long yellow braids. Suzy named her Betsy, and carried the doll with her everywhere. When she rode the bus, Betsy sat next to her. When she went to a restaurant for lunch, Betsy went too and sat in a little doll's chair on the table. The waitresses talked to Betsy and pretended to take her order.

One day, Betsy's head popped off and couldn't be popped back in place. Suzy was devastated and begged her parents to find a way to fix Betsy. Suzy's mother remembered hearing about a woman in town who fixed broken dolls. The doll doctor lived in a frame house with a glassed-in front porch. A sign on the door said, "Doll Hospital."

The glassed-in porch served as a doll infirmary. Hundreds of doll pieces filled shelves lining the walls. One shelf was covered with nothing but arms, one with legs, one with heads, and one with bodies. One shelf had bins of small doll parts, including eyes. On the lowest shelves were dozens of dolls in various stages of repair.

In the middle of the floor was an "examining table". A huge doll with a broken leg rested there, in the process of being fixed. Betsy was placed on this table, while the doll doctor examined her carefully. Suzy was assured that Betsy could be fixed, but she had to be left at the doll hospital for several days. Betsy was placed on an empty spot on the shelf, with an identification card attached to her listing Suzy's name and telephone number.

A few days later Suzy went back to the doll hospital, and there was Betsy, as good as new. Her head was on securely, and her face and body were clean and fresh-smelling. Suzy looked around for the gigantic doll with the broken leg, but she was nowhere in sight. On the shelves, however, were several new dolls, waiting for their turn to be fixed.

A P. XXXV/XXXV

Norman Rockwell

Doctor and Doll (1929) 99

The Dolls' Wardrobe

Julia probably had the best-dressed dolls in town. Every Christmas her grandmother made a beautiful new dress for Julia's favorite doll. Aunt Ruth knit sweaters for Julia's dolls, matching sweaters she had knit for Julia when she was a baby. Julia herself had started making clothes for her dolls by cutting out material, making a hole in top to slip the material over the doll's head, and typing a ribbon around the waist.

Once a year, Julia's grandmother borrowed Julia's old doll clothes and mended, washed, and ironed them, replacing any lost buttons or frayed ribbons. When Julia came over to visit her grandmother, she would find the clothes, looking cleaned and starched, lined up on her grandmother's table.

Julia saved her allowance for six months to buy a doll dress she had seen in the toy store. It was a long, glittery dress, with a black velvet vest and puffed sleeves that could be worn down or pushed up. Julia thought it was the most beautiful dress she had ever seen, and wished that she could have a dress like it herself someday.

Most of Julia's dolls came with tiny, black, rubbery shoes, which fell off their feet easily, never to be seen again. Julia had a whole collection of unmatched dolls' shoes; her mother joked that the missing shoes must be in the same place as the socks that always got misplaced on wash day.

From time to time, Julia stopped to see if Mr. Samuels, the shoemaker, had any used heels that Julia could play hopscotch with. She was usually carrying a favorite doll, and one day Mr. Samuels noticed that the doll's little black shoes had fallen off. The next time Julia stopped by Mr. Samuels' shop, he had a surprise waiting for her. He had made a new pair of tiny shoes for her doll, ones that could be securely tied on so they wouldn't fall off.

Cobbler Studying Doll's Shoe (1921)

The Doll Princess (1915)

The Doll House

When Suzy's grandmother came to visit, she brought the biggest doll Suzy had ever seen. The doll was almost as tall as Suzy, with a straw hat, blond curls, eyes that opened and shut, and outstretched arms. She came with her own comb and brush, and a tiny patent leather pocketbook.

Suzy liked playing school with the new doll, because she was large enough to sit in a chair and look like a real child. But her favorite dolls for everyday play were much smaller, and had many different outfits and furnishings to go with them. Her favorite had long, thick black hair and a beautiful face that reminded Suzy of *Rebecca of Sunnybrook Farm*, which she had just finished reading. Suzy decided to cut the doll's hair into a pixie cut, the newest hair fashion. Unfortunately, when cut, the doll's thick hair became thin and scraggly, and bald spots appeared on her scalp. Suzy couldn't understand what had gone wrong.

One day, a few days before Suzy's birthday, she found her father in the basement building a new bookcase for Philip's bedroom, or so he said. When Suzy went downstairs on her birthday, she found that the bookcase had been transformed into a huge house for her dolls. It had two floors, with three rooms on each floor, a deck, and a patio. There were windows in each room, and a front door that swung open and shut. The house had wheels so it could be rolled from room to room, or into her closet for storage. Her parents had filled the house with special furniture, just the right size for her dolls. There were wooden bunk beds in the bedroom, a pink tub in the bathroom, and a green sofa that rolled out into a bed in the living room. The kitchen had miniature appliances, including a sink that really worked if Suzy filled up its small storage area with water.

Suzy's doll house became a favorite of the neighborhood girls, who gathered in Suzy's room to rearrange the doll house furniture, or help the dolls deal with the pressing issues of being first-time homeowners.

Mother Sending Children Off to School (1919)

Chapter 6
School

The First Day of School

The best part about the beginning of a new school year was going to the five and ten to buy school supplies. There was something wonderful about choosing from rows of notebooks, folders, and different colored markers. The school supplies represented a new, clean start for the children. This year, they promised, they wouldn't doodle all over their notebooks or chew the erasers off their pencils. This was a new start.

The children on Chilton Road went to sleep early the night before school started. Their mothers wanted them to be "fresh" for the first day of class. The children dressed in nicer clothes than usual on that first day, because their mothers wanted them to make a good impression on their new teachers. The teacher received many apples and bouquets of freshly-picked wildflowers on this day.

The newness of school wore off quickly, and by the end of the first day the children had already adapted to the new teachers and the new routines. Old friends had resurfaced, as had old habits—despite their resolutions, they had doodled on their new notebooks and chewed an eraser off one of their new pencils.

The Spelling Bee

Once a year, the children at Hamilton Elementary School participated in a school spelling bee. First, each class held its own spelling bee and picked a winner. Then, the class winners competed against one other, and finally, a school winner was chosen. The school winner competed against winners from the other elementary schools in the area.

Marsha hated spelling bees. She was good enough not to get eliminated immediately, but not good enough to go the distance. Her teacher told the children stand in a line at the front of the classroom, in front of the blackboards. Starting at one end of the line, each child took a turn trying to spell a word. The teacher said the word twice, enunciating very carefully. Then the child spelled the word. If he was incorrect, he sat down, and that was that. If he was correct, he continued to stand in line and wait for his next word. The good spellers stood for a long time.

This process was torture for Marsha. Her stomach felt sick and her legs wobbly when her turn was near. "Please, let me get an easy word," she'd pray to herself. Although she wanted to succeed, part of her wanted to fail, so she could sit down and be put out of her misery. She leaned forward and counted how many more children there were until her turn.

Marsha was relieved when she spelled her first word correctly, thus saving her from the embarrassment of being the first child to sit down. Marsha was convinced that Johnny Pierson misspelled his word on purpose, so he could sit and read comic books when the teacher wasn't looking. Marsha made it through four rounds before being eliminated. She didn't envy Debby Hiatt, the winner, because Debby's prize was to compete in yet another spelling bee.

Cousin Reginald Spells Peloponnesus (1918)

School Play (1918)

The School Play

School plays were fun for the children but a lot of work for the parents, who were expected to sew the costumes and help make the props. Children whose mothers were expert sewers appeared in elaborate costumes that were the envy of the other children. Suzy's mother couldn't sew at all, and Suzy had to piece her costumes together from old clothes that were stored in the basement.

The teachers tried to pick plays that had enough speaking parts for each child in the class, but inevitably some parts were juicier than others. Suzy's class performed skits filled with songs about folk heroes. She was the narrator, and got to wear a small microphone around her neck. Her teacher said she gave Suzy the part as narrator because she had a good speaking voice.

William's class performed a play about pirates. William got to wear his pirate's eye patch and say, "Yo ho ho" in a sinister manner. Paul Miner was a little wild, as usual, and started jumping around more than he was supposed to, swinging his sword. The children didn't know whether to laugh or be mad at him for messing up their play.

Little things always went wrong during these school plays. Someone always forgot his lines, and had to be coached from backstage. A prop suddenly toppled over in the middle of a serious scene, causing giggles from the audience and temporary confusion among the actors. Some children delivered their lines so softly that no one could hear, except the other children on stage.

The parents, sitting on uncomfortable folding chairs in the auditorium, were charmed by the way their children looked on stage, looking so familiar yet so different with their makeup and costumes on.

Report Card (1953)

The Report Card

Four report cards were sent home each school year. The children brought the report cards home in yellow envelopes, got their parents' signatures, and returned them to school the next day. For the good students, report card day meant they could go home confident of pleasing their parents and perhaps of being given a special treat. For the bad students, report card day was a time to be dreaded. Paul Miner's report card was so bad once that he tried to forge his father's signature on it, but the school principal recognized the difference in handwriting.

Sometimes, report cards carried unpleasant surprises, like the time Philip, who was generally an "A" student, got a "D" in handwriting. He was scared to show the grade to his father, but his father laughed and said that handwriting was a a hard thing to accomplish well unless you had the knack.

Marty usually did well on his report cards, but one semester he received a low grade in science. He was mortified, and he was embarrassed to show the report card to his parents. The day the report card was sent home, Marty didn't take it out of his book bag. At school the next day, Marty told his teacher that he had forgotten to bring the report card back. The next evening, he waited for his father to finish reading the newspaper, and then pulled out the card. He realized that he was going to cry; Marty was embarrassed that he always cried when he tried to discuss things that were very important to him. His father looked at the report card and asked why the grade in science was so low. Marty said he didn't know, that he was just having trouble understanding this particular unit in science. His father put his arm on Marty's shoulder and said, "It doesn't matter what grade you get, as long as you try to do your best. If this was the best you could do this time, than that's good enough for me." That was the first time Marty really understood that he didn't have to be perfect for his parents to love him and be proud of him. His father might not have been perfect either, but Marty thought he was the best father in the whole world.

The Black Eye

Marsha was friendly with most of the children in her class, but she couldn't stand Roz Lester. The trouble between Marsha and Roz started way back in kindergarten. Jay's mother, who was very artistic, made silhouettes of the children and mounted them on big, red, construction paper hearts. Mrs. Feldon, their kindergarten teacher, held up each silhouette and told the children to guess which one was theirs; then they could take the pictures home to give to their parents. Roz and Marsha had both been wearing their hair in a pony tail the day the silhouettes were made, and their pictures looked remarkably alike. Mrs. Feldon teased Marsha that she was going to end up taking Roz's silhouette home to her mother instead of her own, but Marsha didn't think it was funny. She didn't want her picture looking so much like Roz's.

Marsha's animosity toward Roz grew when Roz managed to grow long, dagger nails while Marsha's were bitten down to the quick. Once, Roz had run her nails down Marsha's arm, making an ugly scratch.

The two girls always seemed to be competing with each other. They were the last two left in the school hopscotch tournament; they vied against each other for the part of Evelyn in the school play; they both had a crush on Jeffrey Konig.

Their anger toward each other finally erupted on the playground one day. The class was playing dodge ball, and Marsha threw the ball much harder than necessary directly at Roz. Roz came up and punched Marsha in the eye, giving her a black eye. They were sent, one at a time, to the principal's office. The principal said he was very disappointed in Marsha. Marsha was very disappointed too—disappointed that she hadn't hit Roz harder.

Girl with Black Eye (1953)

113

Woman at Vanity (1933)

Chapter 7
Rites of Passage

To Be Sixteen

Julia's family went to Philadelphia to visit relatives. Cousin Laura was sixteen, and Julia thought she was beautiful. Laura had chin-length hair that curled gently in toward her face; Julia's own hair was straight as a pin. Julia studied Laura carefully as she got ready for a date, so that she could duplicate Laura's beauty regime when she returned home.

Laura had a small table in her room, which she converted into a vanity by covering it with frilly, pink material and hanging a mirror over it. Sometimes, Laura let Julia sit on the stool in front of the vanity and play with her makeup. Julia put on red lipstick, and made round circles of rouge on her cheeks. She painted her finger and toe nails with Laura's pink polish.

Once, Laura rolled Julia's hair in curlers and brushed it out for her, so that it curled softly in toward her face, just like Laura's. It looked beautiful at first, but after a couple hours her hair was back to its usual straggly self.

In her day-dreams, Julia was sixteen and looked just like Laura. Her freckles were gone, her tilted-up nose had straightened, and her head was covered with soft, gentle curls.

Younger Doesn't Have to Mean Shorter

It was hard being a younger brother. Matthew got to buy new clothes, but William wore nothing but Matthew's hand-me-downs. William liked all the same sports as Matthew, but he was much smaller and couldn't run as fast, or hit the ball as hard. Matthew was even allowed to stay up later than William.

The worst was that William felt he would never catch up. After his birthday came in May, he was only two years younger than Matthew. But then Matthew's birthday came along in September, and they were three years apart again.

William thought that because he was younger, he would always be smaller than Matthew. But his mother said that a younger person wasn't necessarily shorter than an older person. Look at Steven, she'd say, he's taller than you are and a whole year younger.

William had certain goals that required getting taller. He wanted to be able to reach the overhead light in the den. He wanted to be closer to the basketball net. He wanted to reach the toys on the top shelf of the closet without having to drag a chair over.

His mother recorded William's growth by making marks on his bedroom wall. William could see the marks climbing up the wall, indicating the two-year-old William, the three-year-old William, and so on. He could see that he was making progress. Sometimes, when he was alone in his room, he stood against the wall and twisted his head around to try to see if he had grown since his mother had made the last mark. This year, he had already grown three inches. William was hopeful that not only would he be taller than Matthew someday, but taller than his dad too.

He's Going to Be Taller Than Dad (1939)   117

Missing Teeth

One fall, it seemed as if every child on Chilton Road was missing a tooth. Both of Suzy's front teeth came out, within a week of one another. They had been a little loose for some time, never seeming to get any looser. Suzy forgot about them, until one day she tried to eat an apple and couldn't. It turned out her teeth had suddenly gotten extremely loose.

The next day at school, Suzy had trouble concentrating on her work because she was busy pushing on her teeth with her colored marker. By the time she got home from school, one tooth was hanging at an angle. When she wiggled the tooth, it made a noise that made her mother wince. By the time her father got home from work, the tooth was hanging by a thread. He wiggled the tooth a few times gently, then gave a harder tug, and the tooth was out.

The next day Suzy went up to her teacher and smiled broadly, waiting for her to comment on the new gap. Her teacher didn't notice the missing tooth at first, because she was so accustomed to seeing toothless children.

Matthew lost his first tooth the day his friend Tom moved out of town. Matthew and his family helped Tom's parents pack up their belongings and clean their house. When Tom's mother hugged Matthew goodbye, she said she bet his tooth would be out by the time they saw him next. Matthew was teary as they drove away.

That night, right before bedtime, his tooth fell out. Matthew asked his mother to write something for him. He dictated, "August the 4th. Today was a special day. I was sad because my good friend moved away, and happy because I finally lost my first tooth."

Girl Missing Tooth (1957)

119

The Diary

Suzy gave Marsha a diary for her birthday. It was pink, with the words "My Diary" across the front. The diary had a gold lock, with a tiny gold key on a white ribbon. It was Marsha's favorite present.

Before bedtime, Marsha wrote the day's entry into her diary. "Friday. Went to school. Got a B on the math test. Jeffrey K. smiled at me." Some days, she couldn't think of anything to write and just put, "Nothing much happened today." When she slept over a friend's house, she took the diary with her. They would lie on their beds and read each other selected entries from their diaries.

Marsha liked the secrecy of the diary. She had recently started demanding privacy at home, although privacy was hard to come by in a house with so many siblings. She kept the diary locked, and hid the key in her sewing box. She told secrets to her diary that she would never dare tell her family.

One day, her brother Robert discovered the tiny key in Marsha's sewing box. He unlocked the diary and began to read. Marsha found him sitting at her vanity, absorbed in her diary, with a smirk on his face. She was furious, and mortified. Marsha searched her room for new hiding places for the key and diary. She hung notes outside her door that said, "Keep out, you'll stunt my emotional growth."

About half the pages in the diary were filled up when Marsha lost interest in it. It had gotten tiresome trying to think up something to say every night. The diary remained, forgotten, in its hiding place for years before Marsha came across it while rearranging her room. Marsha felt wistful reading her words of a few years earlier and remembering that young Marsha, who didn't exist any more. She also felt glad, however, that she had finished with that stage in her life, and that it no longer mattered if Jeffrey K. smiled at her or not.

Boy Reading Sister's Diary (1942)

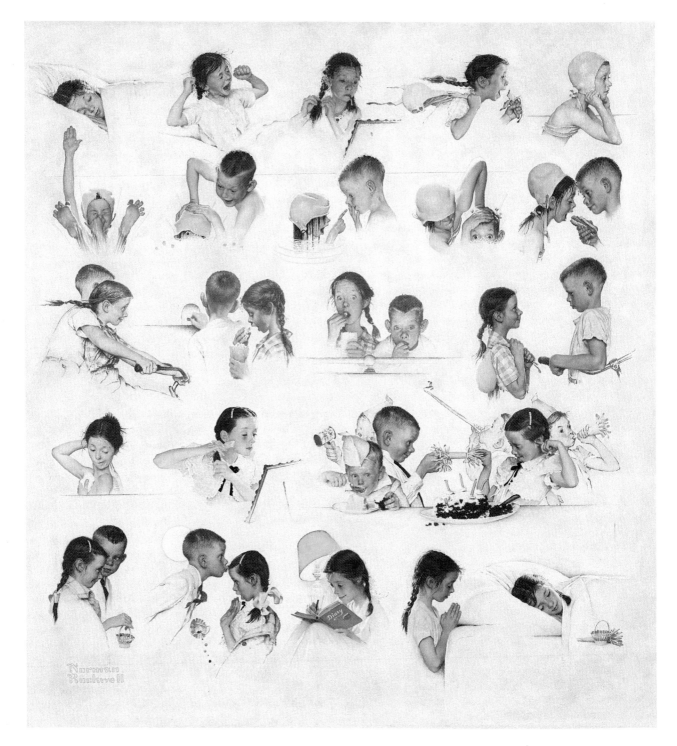

Day in the Life of a Little Girl (1952)

Growing Up

In the spring, Marty's parents painted their house a light tan color. Without the bright green paint, the house looked bare, like a child who had forgotten to finish dressing that morning. The saplings on the hill in front of William's, Matthew's, and Julia's house had grown so tall that their house could no longer be seen from the road.

These weren't the only changes on the street that spring. The children of Chilton Road were growing up. Butch began shaving that spring. He had been contemplating his first shave for weeks, and finally got up the nerve. He hoped that after shaving his beard would grow in thicker and "more manly." No one noticed the difference in Butch's face after his shave, but they did notice that he had suddenly developed the habit of stroking his chin constantly.

William lost the last of his baby fat and grew lean and muscular. He could now keep up with the older children and, while still smaller than they were, was fast and strong.

Suzy no longer looked like a tomboy. She stopped wearing her hair in braids, and playing football with the boys. She went by herself on the train to visit her aunt, wearing a new dress with a white cummerbund. For the first time, her mother let her wear stockings instead of white anklets, which made her feel very grown up. Her aunt was astonished when, instead of a little girl, she saw a young lady descend from the train.

The Chilton Road Gang still spent time together, playing games or just enjoying each other's company. Increasingly, however, they were pulled away from Chilton Road by outside interests; they had parties to go to, school friends to meet, and an ever-increasing number of after-school and weekend activities. Like the old oak tree in the Miller's back yard, the children were anchored to Chilton Road but were branching out in all directions, beyond the boundaries of their home base.

Picture Credits: